Just Handwritin

Pre-cursive Handwriting Prog

Senior Infants

educate.ie

Authors: Catherine Mangan and Marie Westlake
Editor: Susan McKeever
Design: Philip Ryan Graphic Design
Illustration: Stephanie Dix
© 2012 Educate.ie, Castleisland, County Kerry, Ireland.
ISBN: 978-1-908507-14-3

Printed in Ireland by Walsh Colour Print, Castleisland, County Kerry. Freephone 1800 613 111.

Contents

Introduction

The **Just Handwriting** series consists of:
Just Handwriting: Early Years (3-4 years)
Just Handwriting: Early Years (4-5 years)
Just Handwriting Script: Junior Infants to Second Class. (Includes a practice copy for each class.)
Just Handwriting Cursive: Junior Infants to Sixth Class. (Includes a practice copy for each class from Junior Infants to Second Class.)

The aim of the programme is to enable children to write fluently, comfortably, quickly and legibly. Handwriting is a form of communication and one on which we are often judged.

Remember the Four Ps: Preparation, Pencil Grip, Posture, Practice.

Preparation (Junior Infants to Second Class): The simple, fun 'Let's Get Ready!' exercises help to relax the child mentally and physically and enable them to focus on the planned activity. Encourage the child to draw or trace the 'Giant Sunglasses' before every writing activity. In time, it will become part of their work routine.

Pencil Grip: The correct pencil grip will lead to quick, fluent writing.

Posture: Good posture helps the writing stamina of the child.

Practice: The formation of each letter is clearly illustrated so the child will have a reference that shows him or her how to form each letter, especially if more than one stroke is involved. Handwriting is an essential skill that needs to be taught and fluency only comes with plenty of practice. Practice, practice, practice makes perfect and enables the child to become a confident writer.

Assessment

There is a self-assessment option at the bottom of each page. The child ticks the face that they feel applies to their completion of the page.

Individual Books (Pre-cursive to Cursive Version)

Junior Infants Book: This book focuses on the correct formation of all lowercase letters. The letters are pre-cursive (with 'tails'). This level also includes a practice copy; this focuses on the formation of lowercase letters, and can be used at the teacher's discretion.

Senior Infants and First Class Books: These books focus on the correct formation of all uppercase letters as well as further practice in lowercase. Both books include a practice copy, focusing on capital letters, that can be used at the teacher's discretion.

Second Class Book: In the Second Class book the width of the lines changes from 6mm to 5mm from Page 39 onwards in preparation for third class. All writing exercises are meaningful e.g. recipes, quiz-style questions and answers and interesting facts. (Includes a practice copy.)

Third to Sixth Class (Cursive Writing)

Third Class Book: This is the stage where children are introduced to cursive looped writing. They will discover that many of the lowercase letters are unchanged from those that have been taught already. Most of the remaining letters involve loops. Later in the year the capital letters are introduced.

Fourth Class Book: Now the children begin to write using a pen. An inexpensive cartridge pen with a fine-pointed nib or a fine-pointed fibre pen (not felt) is recommended. Under no circumstances should a biro or a ballpoint pen be used. In fact these types of pens should not be used for writing in any primary school class.

The Fifth Class Book: Lower and uppercase letters are repeated from Pages 3 to 11 to revise, reinforce and provide practice of correct letter formation. The most important writing rules are repeated throughout the book. Pupils should use the same pen suggested in the Fourth Class book. The contents of this book vary from facts, stories and poetry to dictionary exercises and legends.

The Sixth Class Book: Lower and uppercase letters from Pages 3 to 8 provide revision of letter formation. Once again the writing rules are repeated throughout the book. The first half of the book has blue and red lines; the second half of the book has double blue lines for 12 pages and 'copy' lines for the last 12 pages. Pupils are recommended to use the same type of pen as they used in Fourth and Fifth Class. There is a variety of material in this book – factual pieces, legends, riddles, stories and tongue twisters.

Let's Get Ready!

Wake Up!

1. Gently 'wash your face' using your fingers.
2. Tap gently around your eyes.
3. Tug at the top of your ears. Tug at the middle of your ears. Tug at your earlobes.
4. Massage your jaw. Get rid of those yawns.
5. Take a deep breath and lift your shoulders to your ears. Breathe out and drop your shoulders.

Pencil Grip

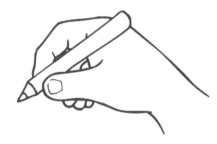

Don't squeeze me! Hold me!
Put your pencil down on the desk. The point of your pencil should be facing your tummy. Bring down your writing hand. Use your thumb and forefinger to pick up your pencil. Push the pencil back into the 'valley' of your hand.

Checklist

This panel appears throughout the book to remind children to: **1.** Wake up!, **2.** Check their posture (chair in, feet down, back straight, don't frown) and **3.** Check their pencil grip.

Wake up!	Posture	Pencil grip

Giant Sunglasses

1. Trace over the 'sunglasses' with your finger.
2. Trace over the 'sunglasses' with your pencil.

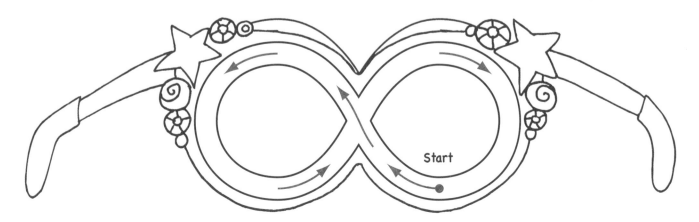

Start

C   O

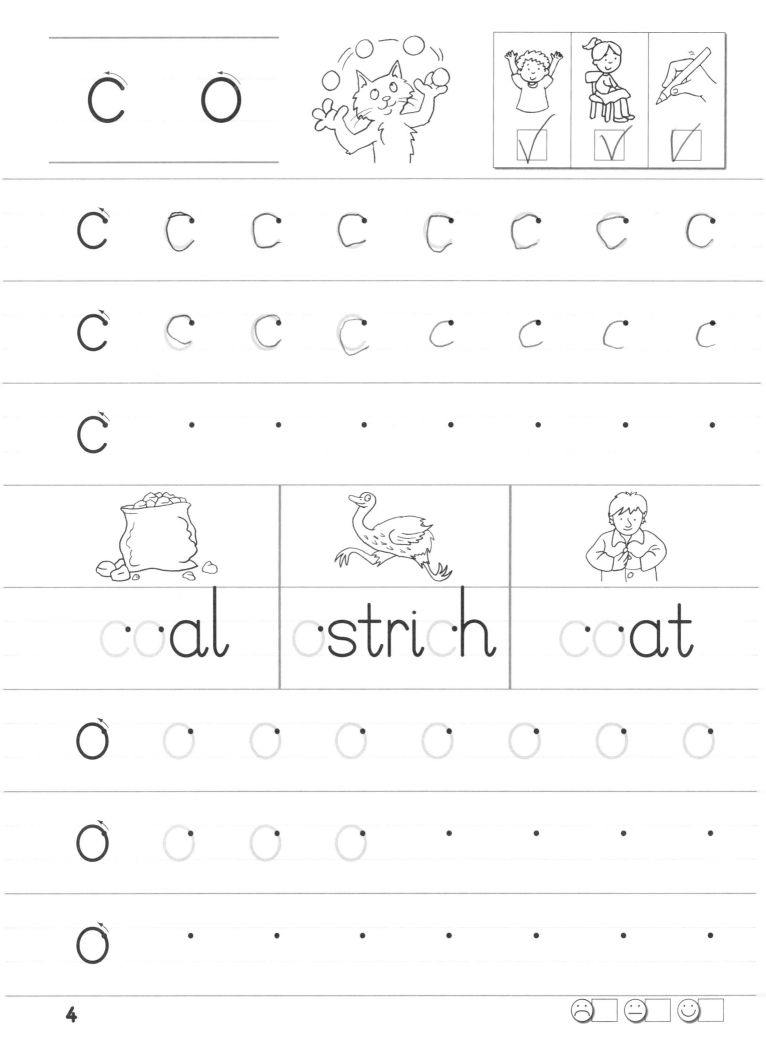

c c c c c c c c c c c c c c c c

c c c c c c c c c c c c c c c c

c c · · · · · · ·

coal | ostrich | coat

o o o o o o o o o o o o o o o o

o o o o o o o · · · ·

o o · · · · · ·

a d

a a a a a a a a a

a a a a

a

card dance add

d d d d d d d d

d d d d

d

5

g q

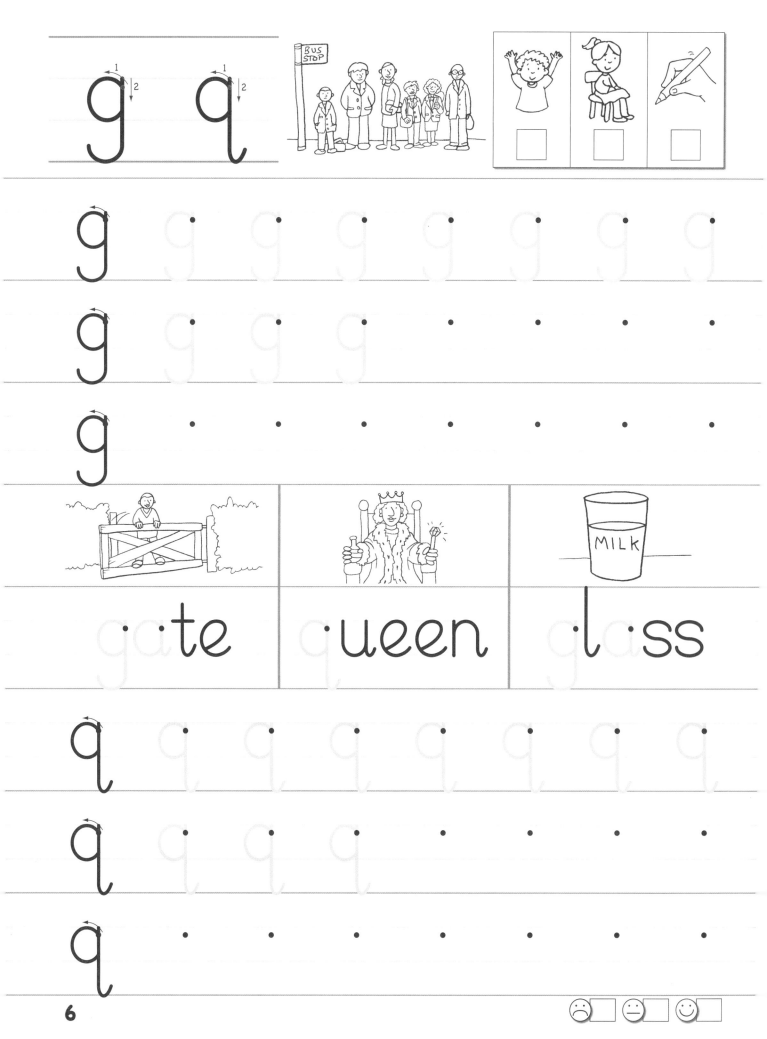

g g g g g g g g g

g g g g

g

gate queen glass

q q q q q q q

q q q

q

u y

u u u u u u u u u

u u u u u

u

truck sunny cry

y y y y y y y y y

y y y y

y

7

coadgquy

c o a d g q u y

c o a d g

y u q g d a o c

y u q g d

c a d o g y q u

c a d o g

d o g u y a c q

d

r h

↓r r r r r r r r r

↓r r r r r r r r

↓r r r r r r r

rain   crash   horse

↓h h h h h h h h h

h h h h h h

h h h h h h

9

n   m

n   n n n n n n n n n n n
n   n n n n n n n n n n n
n   n . . . .

nose   mouse   monkey

m   m m m m m m m m m m m
m   m m m m m m m m m m m
m   m . . . .

s   e

Chair in,
Feet down,
Back straight,
Don't frown.

s   s   s   s   s   s   s   s

s   s   s   s   .   .   .   .

s   .   .   .   .

dress   slipper   snake.

e   e   e   e   e   e   e   e

e   e   e   e   .   .   .   .

e   .   .   .   .

11

jump   sing   jam

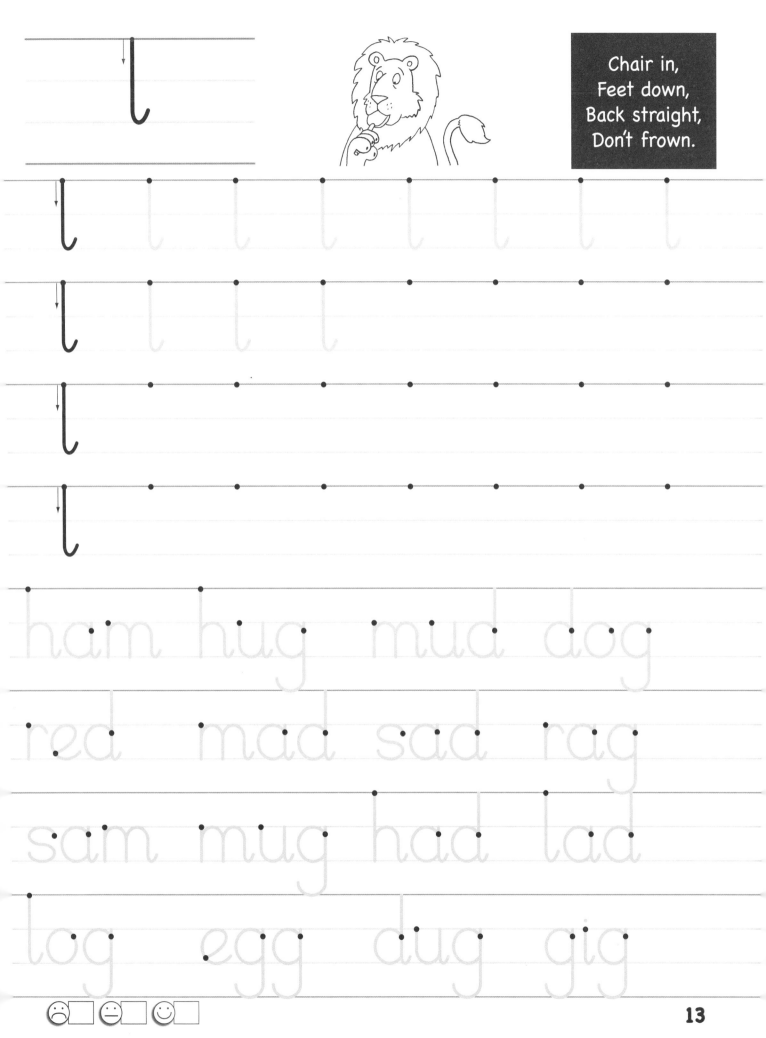

Chair in,
Feet down,
Back straight,
Don't frown.

l l l l l l l l l

l l l l l l l l l

ham hug mud dog

red mad sad rag

sam mug had lad

log egg dug gig

13

t b

t t t t t t t t

t t t t t

t

tank   bat   boat

b b b b b b b

b b b b

b

p k

k k k k k k k k k

k k k k

k

peck   kite   kitten

p p p p p p p p p

p p p p

p

f

f f f f f f f

f f f f f f f

f f f f f f f

five   raft   fire

a d g e r i s p

a d g e

a d g

Words

dog

duck

hen

b.

b

s

fish

p

r

m

17

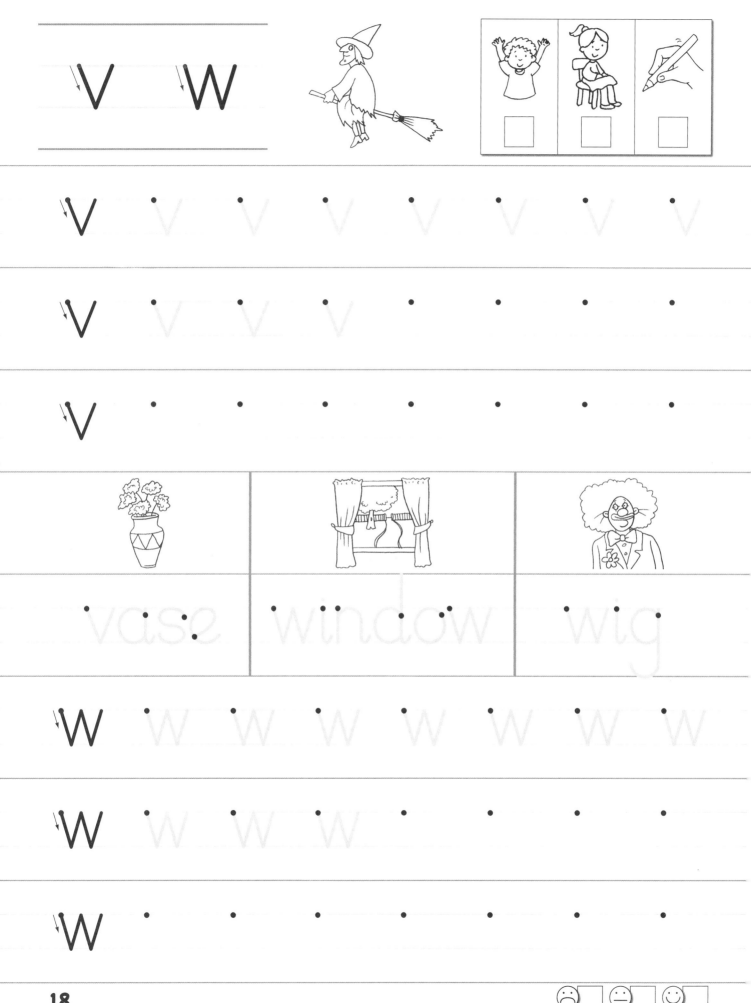

V W

V V V V V V V V

V V V V V V V V

V V V V V V V V

vase window wig

W W W W W W W W

W W W W W W W W

W W W W W W W W

18

X Z

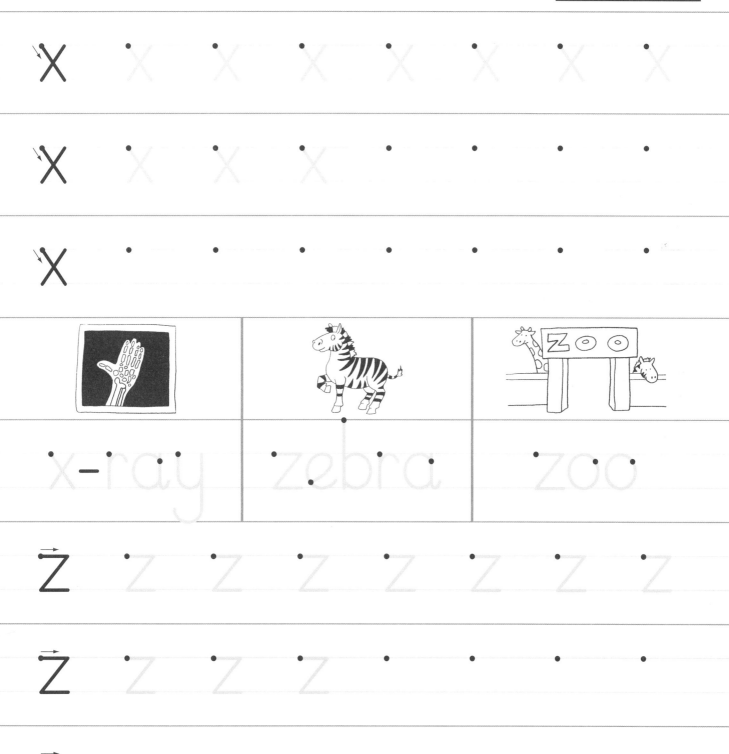

X   x   x   x   x   x   x   x

X   x   x   x

X

x-ray   zebra   zoo

Z   z   z   z   z   z   z   z

Z   z   z   z

Z

19

Words

cat

desk

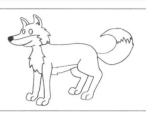

fox

b • •

t • •

oo •

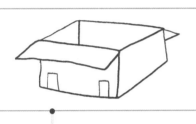

b •

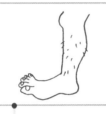

m • •

c • •

t •

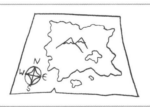

l • •

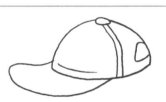

b • •

C c

Curve around the handle of the cup.

C C C C C C C C C C

C C C C

C

Cathy Caleb Carlo

C C c C c C c C c

C C c C c C c

C C c C c

C

21

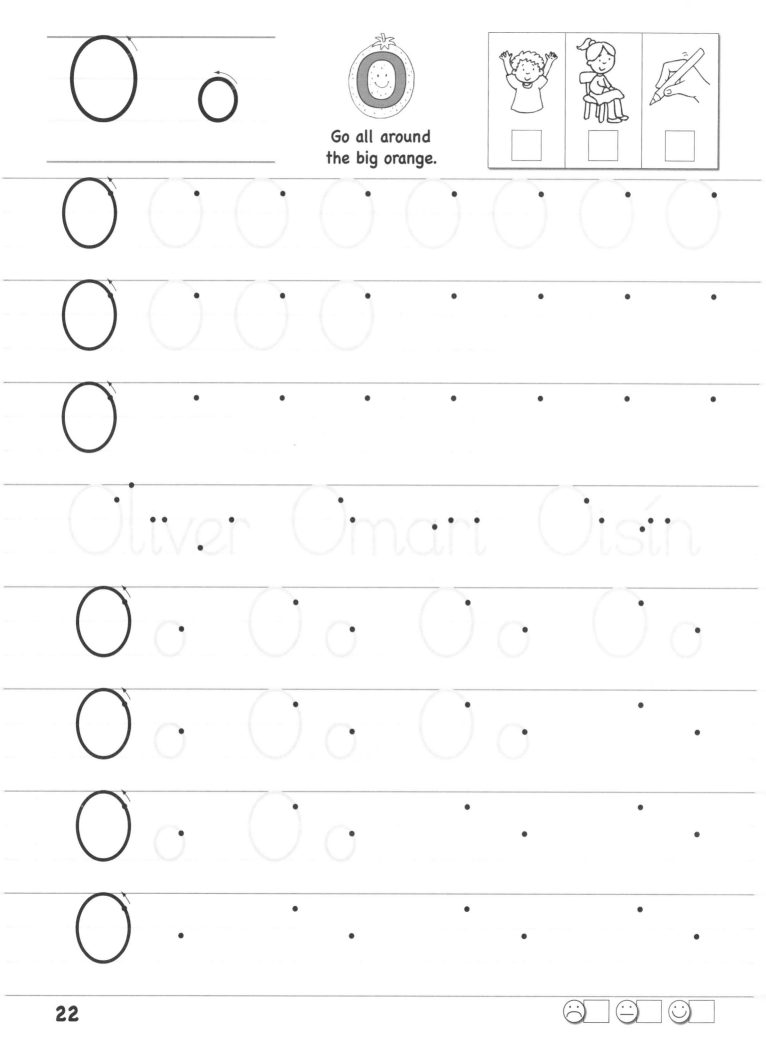

Go all around
the big orange.

Oliver Omari Oisín

S s

Start at the swan's head. Go down his long neck. Sit him on the lake.

S · S · S · S · S · S · S ·

S · S · S · S · S ·

S · · · · · · ·

Sam   Sarah   Sofia

S · S s   S s   S s

S · S s   S s   S s   ·

S · S s   S s   · · ·

S · · · · · · ·

23

Z z

Go across his head.
Go down his neck.
Go across his body.

Z Z Z Z Z Z Z Z Z Z

Z Z Z Z Z

Z

Zach   Zoe   Zara

Z z   Z z   Z z   Z z

Z z   Z z   Z z

Z z   Z z

Z

COSZ

Chair in,
Feet down,
Back straight,
Don't frown.

Sue and Zoe are pals.

Con and Otto are too.

Off they go.

Off t   g

Sue and Zoe.

S   a   Z

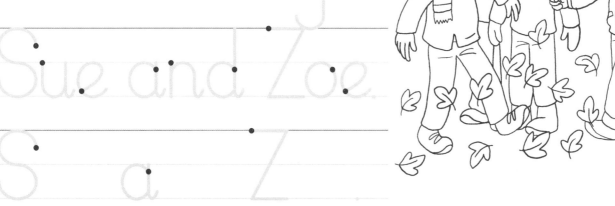

Con and Otto.

C   a   O

25

COSZ

Christmas

C

Santa Claus

S   C

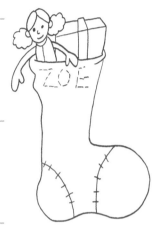

Oliver gets a big ball.

O   g   a   b   b

Zoe gets a big doll.

Z   g   a   b   d

Slide down and up the vampire's tooth.
(If you dare!)

Vera   Vicky   Victor

27

W w

Slide down and up; down
and up the walrus' teeth.

W W W W W W W W W

W W W W

W

William Wendy Wanda

W w W w W w W w

W w W w W w

W

28

I i

Go down his straight body.
Make his antennae. Make his back legs.

Isabel Ian Ita Ivan

Go down to the knee, then
across to the toes.

Liam   Lisa   Louisa

VWIL

VWIL

Vicky   Vince

V   V

Where do you live?

W   d   y   l   ?

I live in Limerick.

It   i   L

I live in Waterford.

It   i   W

VWIL

Liam is from Ireland.
L   i   f   l

Vera is from Italy.
V   i   f   I

Wynn is from Wales.
W   i   f   W

Santa is from Lapland.
S   i   f   L

First make the first post. Then add the bar across. Then make the second post.

Chair in,
Feet down,
Back straight,
Don't frown.

H H H H H H H H H

H H H H

H

Harry   Holly   Hana

H Hh Hh Hh Hh H Hh

H Hh Hh H Hh

H Hh H Hh

H

33

A   a

Draw the first side,
then the second.
Finish with the step.

A A A A A A A A A

A A A A A

A A A A A A A A A

Abbie Aaron Akemi

A A a A a A a A a

A A a A a A a

A A a A a

A

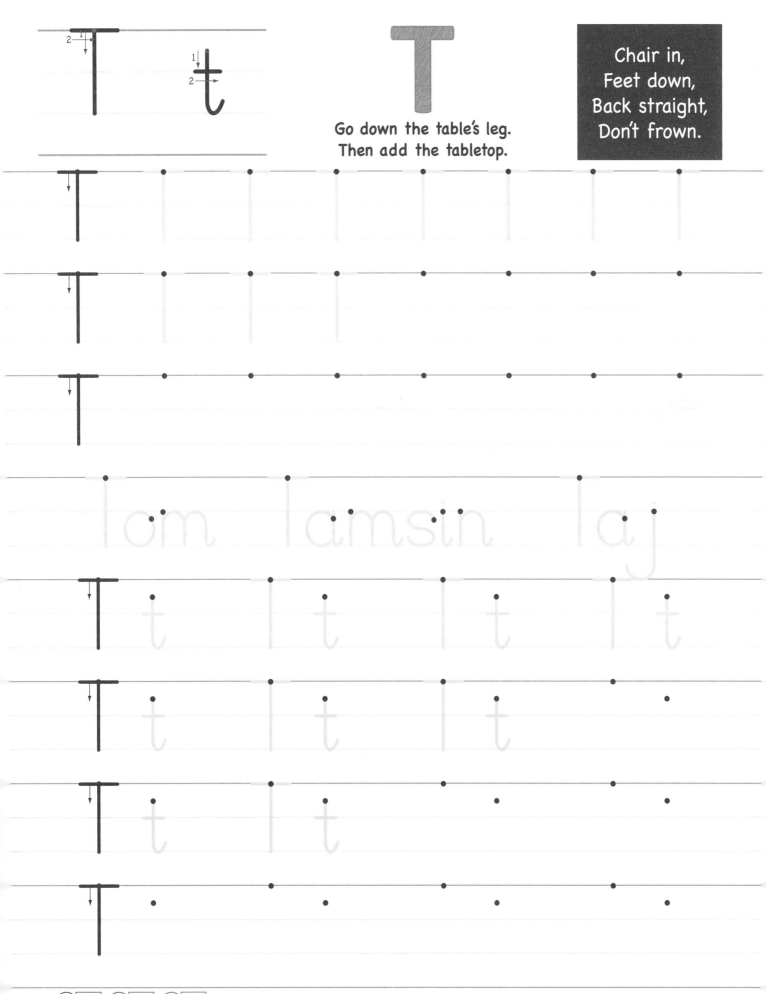

Go down the table's leg.
Then add the tabletop.

Tom   Tamsin   Taj

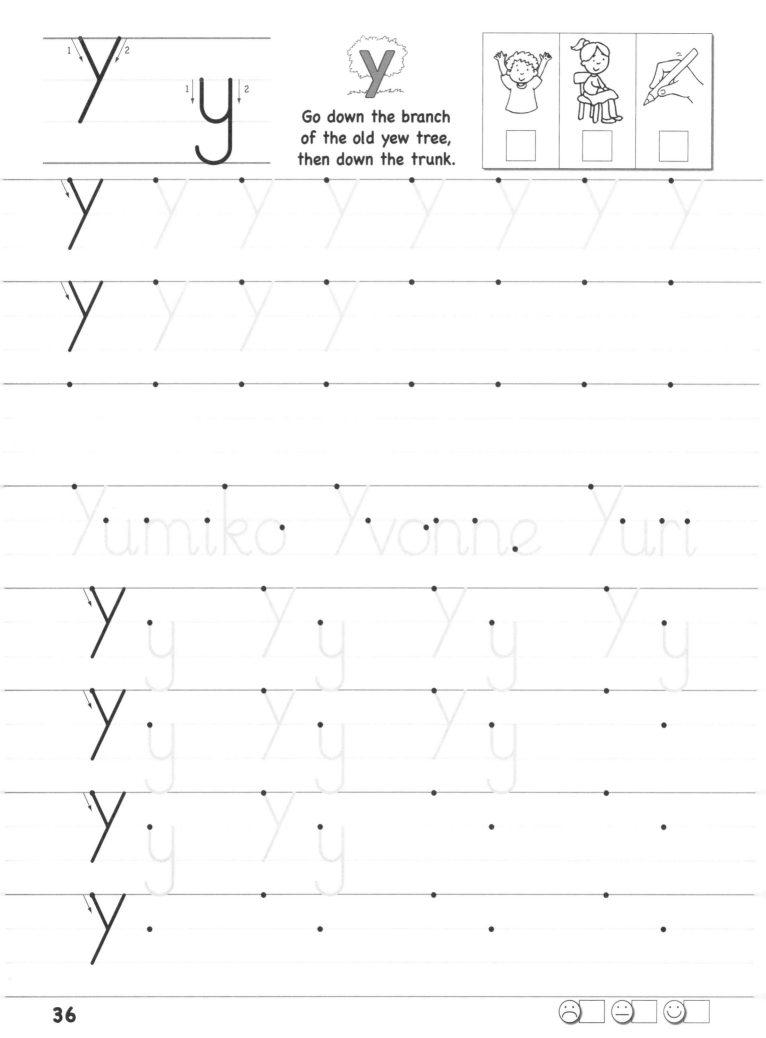

Go down the branch
of the old yew tree,
then down the trunk.

Yumiko   Yvonne   Yuri

HATY

Halloween is here.

Halloween is h

Trick or treat.

T   o   t

Abbie is a black witch.

A   i   a b   w

Yvonne is a white ghost.

Y   i   a w   g

HATY

Abbie scares Harry.

A s H

Yvonne scares Tamsin.

Y s T

Happy
Halloween

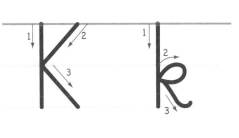

Go down daddy kangaroo's body.
Go in for his arms, and out for his legs.

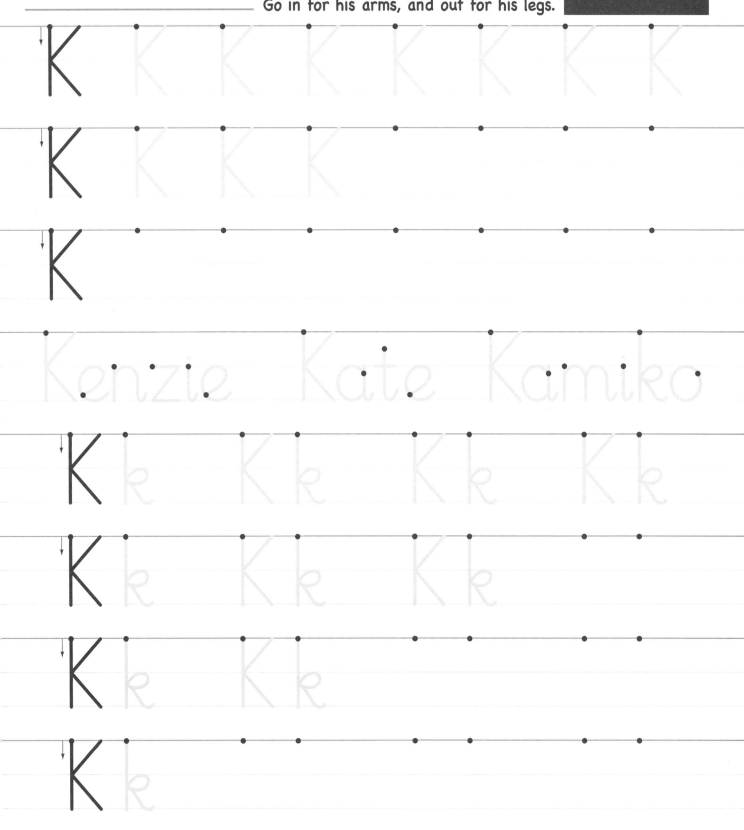

Kenzie   Kate   Kamiko

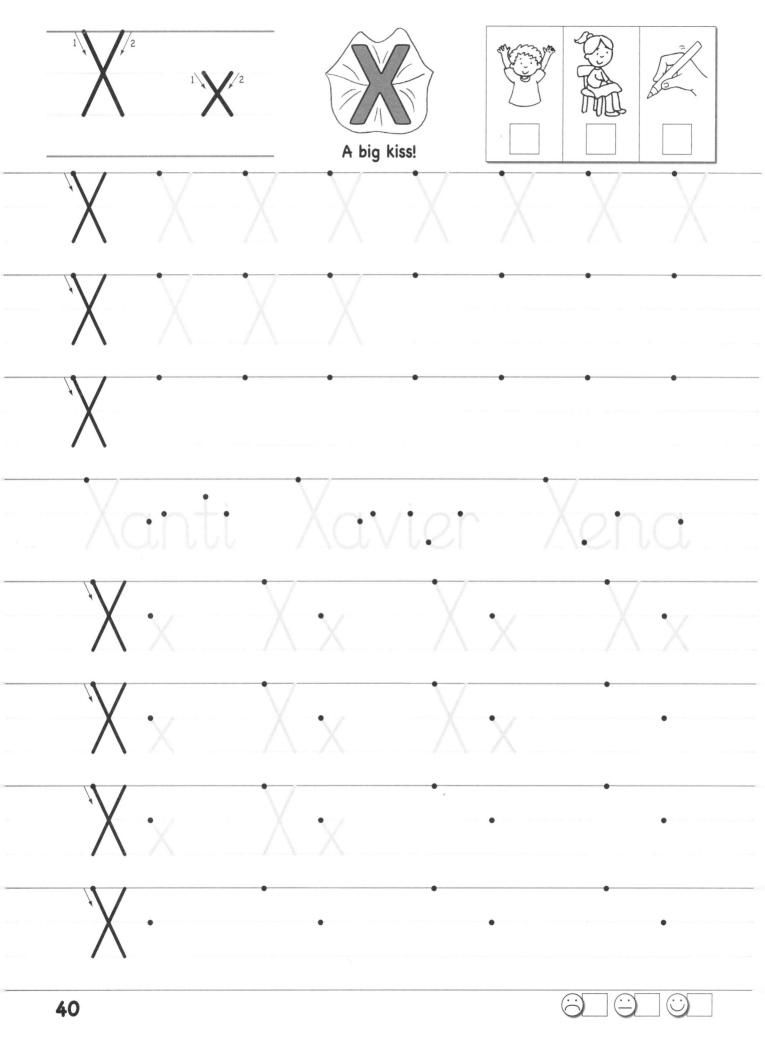

A big kiss!

Xanti   Xavier   Xena

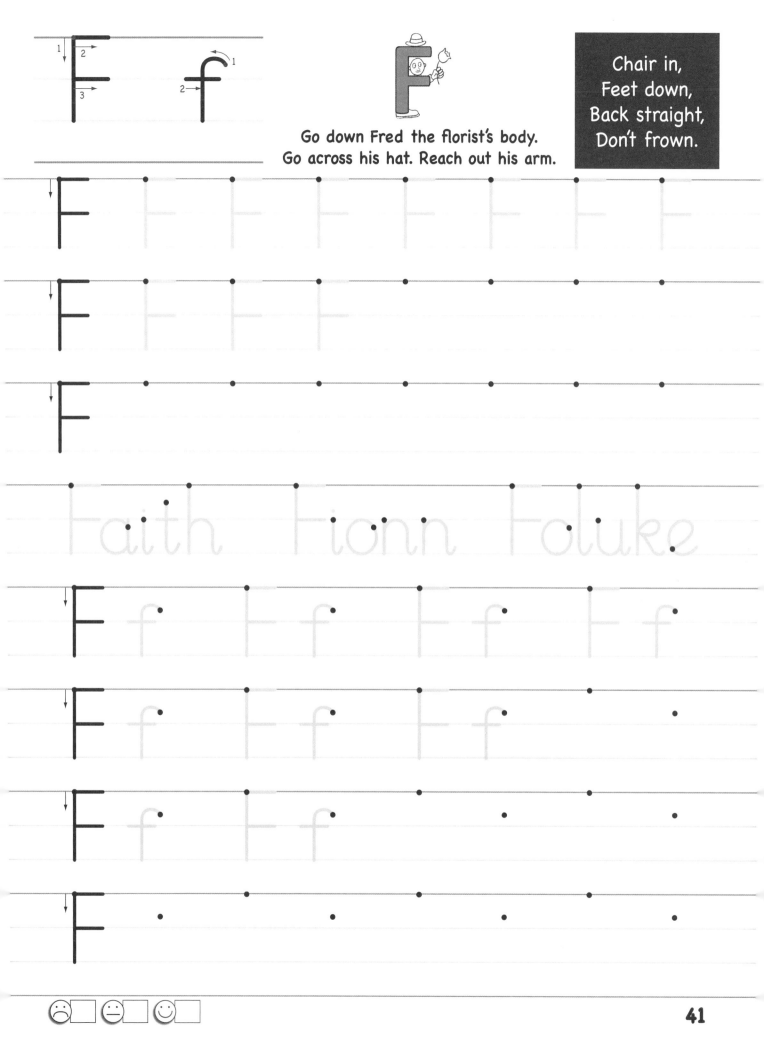

Go down Fred the florist's body.
Go across his hat. Reach out his arm.

Faith Fionn Foluke

E e

Go down the elephant's body. Then go across her trunk and two legs.

E E E E E E E E E

E E E E E E E E E

E E E E E E E E E

Emma Ethan Eriko

Ee Ee Ee Ee

Ee Ee Ee

Ee Ee

E

KXFE

Find the treasure.

F t t

Is it in France?

Is it in Kenya?

Is it in Egypt?

Is it in Finland?

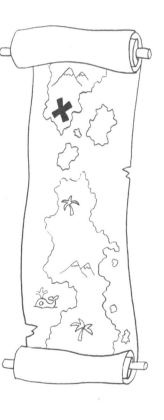

X marks the spot.

X m t s

KXFE

King Edward
K   E

King Francis
K   F

Edward ruled England.
E   r   E

Francis ruled France.
F   r   F

M m

Go down the first
bedpost.
Bend the mattress.
Then go down the
other bedpost.

M M M M M M M M M

M M M M M

M

Mary Makaya Mark

M Mm Mm Mm Mm

M Mm Mm Mm

M Mm Mm

M

45

N n

Go down the billy goat's first horn. Bend it down, and go up the second.

N N N N N N N N

N N N N N

N

Naomi   Niall   Nicola

N n   N n   N n   N n

N n   N n   N n

N n   N n

N

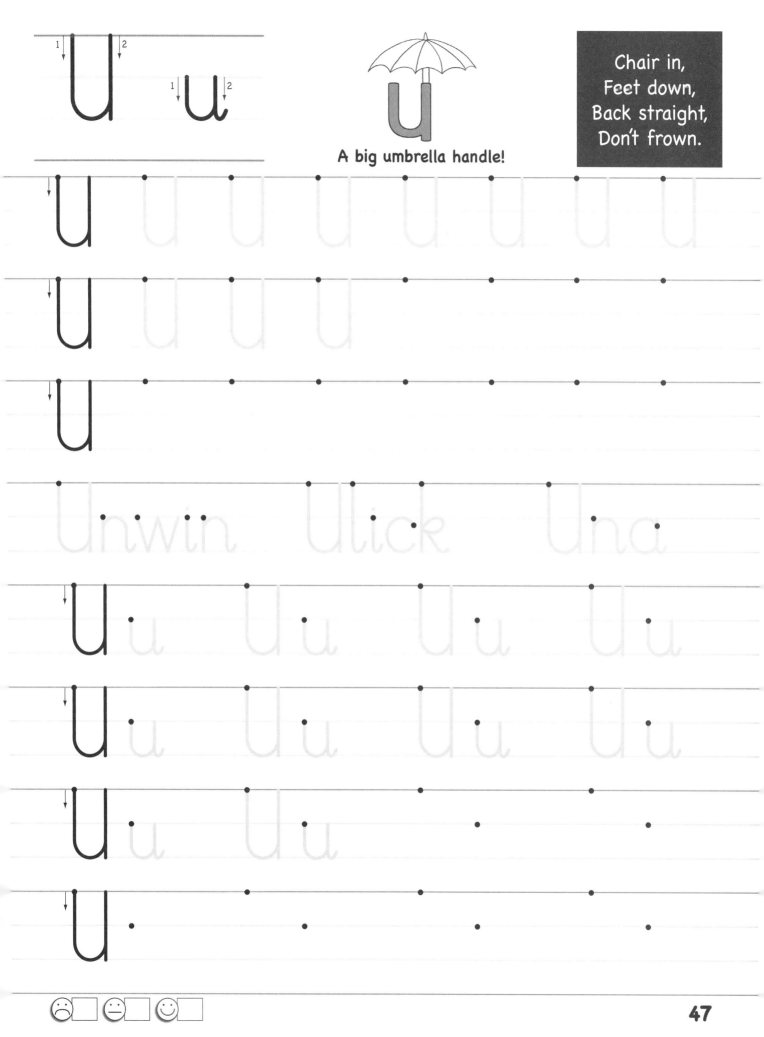

A big umbrella handle!

U U U U U U U U U

U U U U U U U U U

U U U

Unwin   Ulick   Una

U u   U u   U u   U u

U u   U u   U u   U u

U u   U u

U

Jack jumps up. Go down his body, then draw his arms.

Jack Jenny Jayla

MNUJ

Max likes the autumn.

M l t a

Max kicks the leaves.

M k t l

January is in winter.

J i in w

Una loves the snow.

U l t s

MNUJ

March is in the spring

M   i   i   t   s

Nests are full of eggs.

N   a   f   o   e

May is in summertime.

M   i   i   s

Niall made a castle.

N   m   a c

D D d

Go down the door frame
then go around the door.

D D D D D D D D D

D D D D

D

Darren Dylan Deon

D D d D d D d D d

D D d D d D d

D D d D d

D

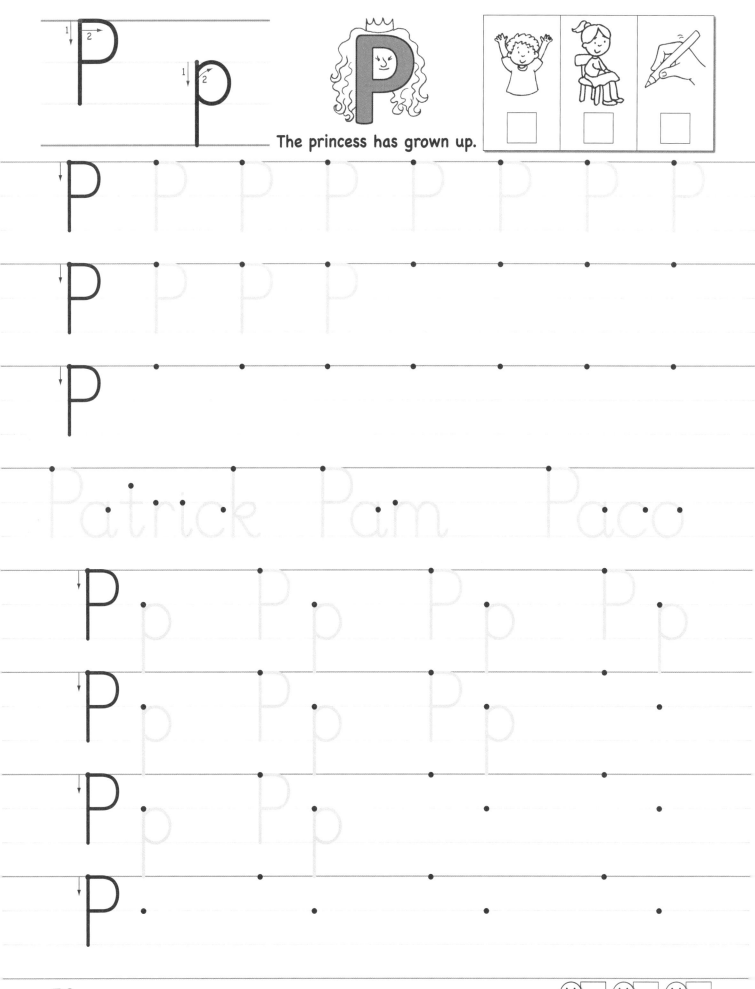

The princess has grown up.

Patrick   Pam   Paco

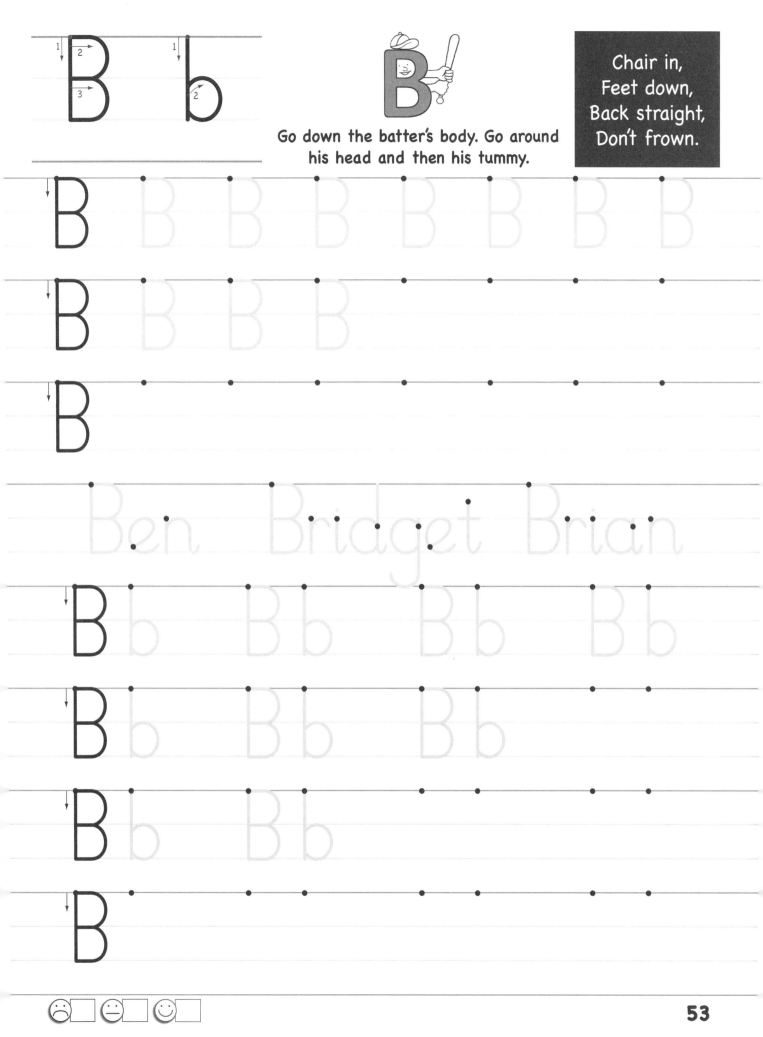

Go down the batter's body. Go around
his head and then his tummy.

B B B B B B B B B

B B B B

B

Ben   Bridget Brian

B Bb   Bb   Bb   Bb   Bb

B Bb   Bb   Bb

B Bb   Bb

B

R r

Go down the rabbit's body,
around his face,
then down the paw.

R R R R R R R R R

R R R R R

R R R R R

Robbie Renata Rhys

R r R r R r R r

R r R r R r

R r R r

R

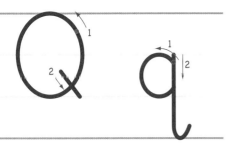

Go all around the queen's carriage,
then down the steps.

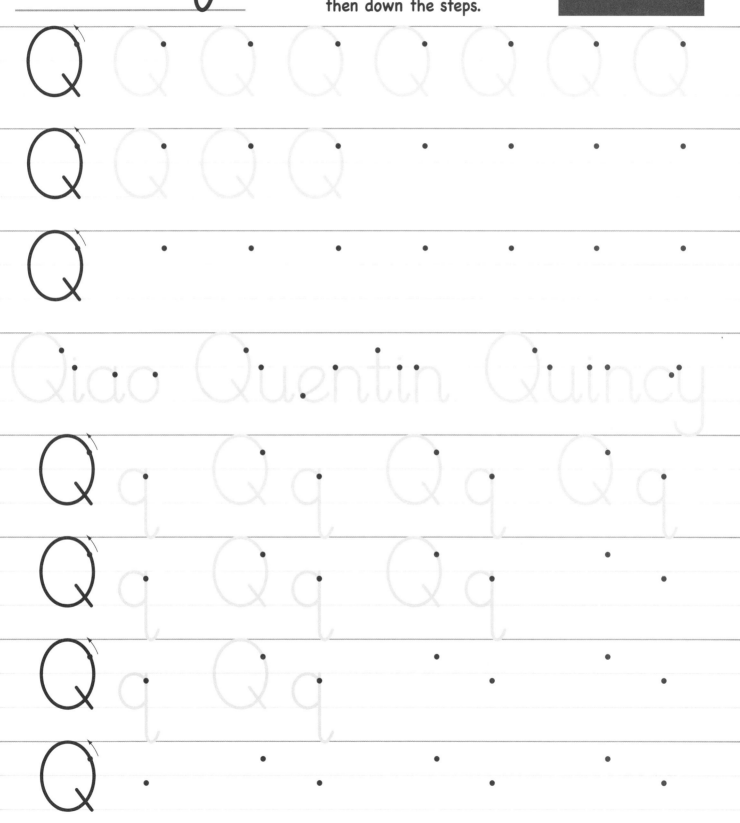

Qiao   Quentin   Quincy

55

G g

G G G G G G G G

G G G G

G

Grace Gavin Gemma

G g G g G g G g G g

G g G g G g G g

G g G g G g

G

DBG

Goldilocks got in.

G g i

Baby Bear cried.

B B c

Daddy Bear growled.

D B g

Goldilocks ran away.

G r a

MPRQ

   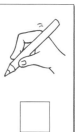

Ron likes Rapunzel.

R   t   R

Mary likes Peter Pan.

M   l   P   P

Mum likes Pinocchio.

M   l   P

Quiet please!

Q   p

58

Numbers 1 2

Chair in,
Feet down,
Back straight,
Don't frown.

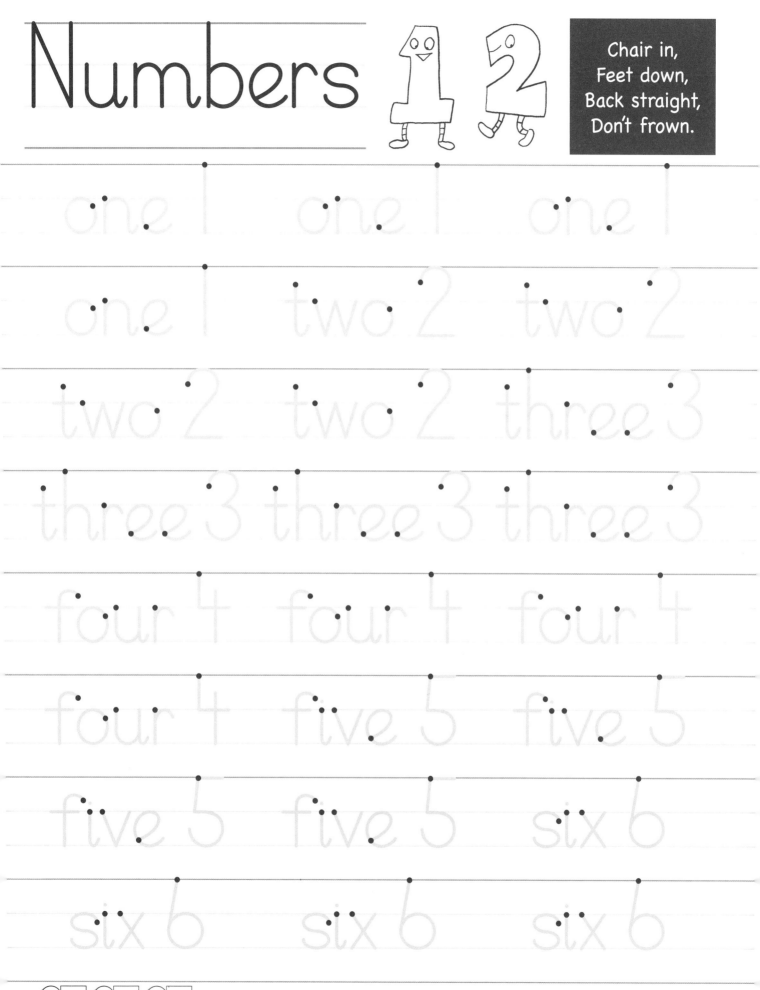

one 1   one 1   one 1

one 1   two 2   two 2

two 2   two 2   three 3

three 3   three 3   three 3

four 4   four 4   four 4

four 4   five 5   five 5

five 5   five 5   six 6

six 6   six 6   six 6

Numbers

seven 7 seven 7 seven 7

seven 7 eight 8 eight 8

eight 8 eight 8 nine 9

nine 9 nine 9 nine 9

ten 10 ten 10 ten 10

1 2 3 4 5 6 7 8 9 10

1 2 3 4 5 6 7 8 9 10

1 2 3 4 5 6 7 8 9 10

Days

Monday

Tuesday

Wednesday

Thursday

Days

Friday

Saturday

Sunday

I like school. I like reading and writing.

Seasons

spring

s

summer

s

autumn

a

winter

w

a A b B c C d D e E
z Z
y Y
x X
w W
v V
u U
t T
s S
r R

I am very good
at writing
small letters
and
capital letters.

Signed

_____

Teacher or parent

f F
g G
h H
i I
j J
k K
l L
m M
q Q p P o O n N

64